Ungrateful Ursula

Book #21 of the Spirit of Truth Storybook Series

By Linda Mason

Ungrateful Ursula
Book #21 of the Spirit of Truth
Storybook Series

Author: Linda C. Mason

Self published by:
Linda C. Mason
P. O. Box 1162
Powhatan, VA 23139
LM.SpiritOfTruth@gmail.com
www.BooksByLMason.com

Color Print:

ISBN-13: 978-1-5356-0755-1

ISBN-10: 1-5356-0755-6

Printed in the United States of America.

Ungrateful Ursula

"I want the blue one! The purple one isn't popular anymore," I told Dad, as I picked out a new head set I wanted to show off at school.

"But don't you have two head sets at home already, Ursula?" Dad asked.

"Yes, but they are old. Grandma got those for me last Christmas. No one is wearing those old styles anymore," I stated, unconcerned.

"Is anything wrong with the old ones? Are they broken?" Dad asked.

"I don't know," I replied. "They are just old. I need new ones now," I insisted as I gave him a stare that indicated how old fashioned he was.

"What about a new pair of shoes too?" I asked, knowing very well that I had plenty of shoes and boots already.

"These boots right here are awesome!" I stated, as I headed over to the boot rack.

As my dad and I stood in the store, waiting to decide on what to buy for my thirteenth birthday, I started thinking about all the things I'd left back at my grandma's house. At one time my dad had also lived there, but when he started traveling a lot, he moved out. Grandma Pearl had always taken very good care of me and allowed me to get just about anything I wanted. I was thirteen years old now, and had to move away from my grandma's to live with my dad because of her declining health. We were only a couple of miles from each other though, so I could go to visit her most anytime I wanted to. Dad had hired a nurse to take care of her now. I really do love her, even though she probably wouldn't think so from the way I acted while living with her.

I never knew my mom, but my dad had been a part of my life along with Grandma Pearl over the years. He had a job that kept him traveling most of the time, so he really couldn't spend the time with me that was necessary to take proper care of me. That's why Grandma Pearl stepped in -- well, up to this point, anyway. I think she always felt a little guilty though, because my mom, who is her daughter, was never in my life. That is probably why she let me have my way most of the time. My motto is *'get as much as you can, while you can.'*

I guess I might be a little selfish and even ungrateful as well; but you know what? I deserve to have everything I want. It's not my fault grown-ups don't know how to raise children. It's not my fault my mother took off and never came back. They owed me whatever I wanted.

Remembering back when I was a lot younger, my dad tried to spend as much time with me as he could. He enjoyed singing and so did I, and we would spend time together singing songs for hours. I miss those times. Over the past few years his job seemed to have kept him gone most of the time. I figured I'd just make up for how much I missed my dad by demanding that my grandma buy me any and everything I wanted. Even though she did, that still never seemed to make me very happy. I pretended around my friends that I was happy, but when I was alone in my room, I didn't feel happy at all. I actually missed those times I used to spend with my dad, and I think I also longed for my mom.

Most often I remember spending a lot of time in my own bedroom, ripping up library books and breaking up expensive toys and electronics my Grandma Pearl bought for me. Who cared if they were broken? Who cared if Grandma Peal had to replace the books with money from her saving's account? I'm not going to spend time worrying about things like that.

Over the last year I would get so mad that I started cutting myself in areas on my body that no one could see. My areas of choice for Cutting were my upper thighs, my stomach, or even my upper arms where I made sure I wore long sleeves when I went out so no one would notice. It seemed as though when I felt the pain of the cut, the pain I felt in my heart from my empty life would go away.

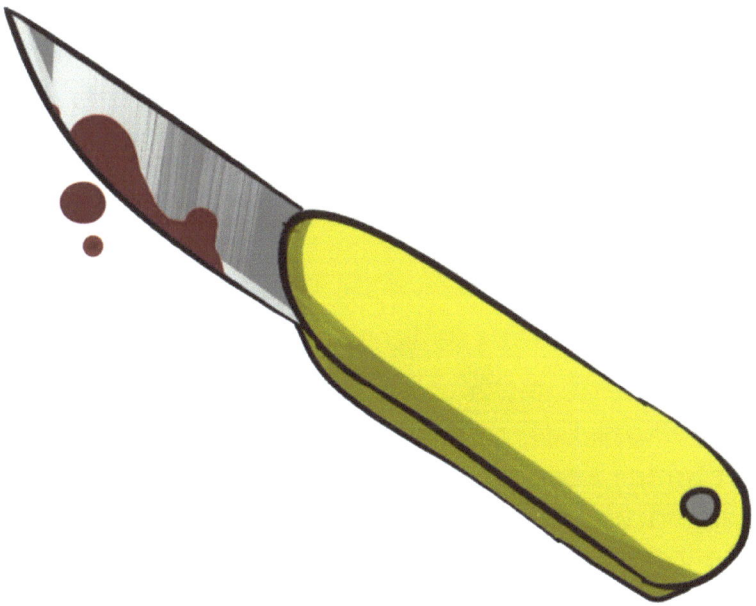

My thoughts returned to the shoe store my dad and I was now in. Would he purchase me anything I wanted, like my Grandma Pearl had?

"Well Dad, are you going to buy me that headset or not? These boots right here will go dandy with my purple outfit, too" I demanded once I had stopped daydreaming of times gone by.

"Since it's your birthday, Ursula, I'll get them this time, but you will have to take care of them" Dad said as he took both items over to the register for check out.

"And when can I start calling my friends to come to my birthday party?" I continued as I helped carry the bags to the car.

"Ursula, we will talk about that birthday party when we get home. OK?" Dad stated with an expression on his face that I really couldn't read.

Dad seemed to have changed a little since we had last spent time together. He seemed more serious -- more mature. He reminded me of a grown-up, who had no intention of allowing a child like me to call the shots. I don't think I was looking forward to our little *'talk'* when we got home.

When we pulled up in the driveway and stopped, I opened the car door immediately and jumped out. I started running up to the front door and Dad got out of the car and called to me.

"Young lady, would you come back and get your bags please?"

"You can get them" I said with a tone I don't think he appreciated.

"Ursula, if you can't take your own packages in, I guess you don't really want them. I can take them back to the store. Which will it be?" He asked.

I stomped back to the car, snatched the bags up, and ran back to the door. As I waited for Dad to unlock the door, I couldn't believe he was treating me like this. That's ok, I thought. I'll fix him. I took my bags to my room and started looking for my pocket knife.

"Ursula!" Dad called out. "Ursula, could you come here for a few minutes?" He continued. I looked at the bags I had thrown on the bed and went to see what he wanted, slamming the bedroom door behind me as I left.

"Ursula, would you please go back to your room, open your bedroom door again, and close it properly," He said in a most calm manner.

"What?!" I yelled, stomping my foot as I spoke.

"Why are you making me do that?" I asked, very irritated by now.

"Ursula, when you come back from shutting your door properly, we need to sit down for a few minutes. We need to discuss setting some ground rules now that you are going to be living with me," Dad said.

"I realize that you've had to grow up without a mother being in your life, and mostly without a father as well. I'm so sorry you've had to grow up mostly alone. I know that your grandma has done the best she knew to do by you, and I'm so grateful she was there to step in for me and your mom; however, I am here now. Honey, you can't continue behaving the way you've grown accustomed to. Excuse me a minute."

8

Dad went into the kitchen and brought back a glass of lemonade for both of us, and then he continued.

"I had a talk with your Grandma Pearl the other day. We discussed you mostly, and your lack of respect for the things she buys for you. Most of your electronics and toys were destroyed by you, almost as soon as you brought them home from the store. She feels that you are doing this intentionally. Your grandma had replaced them for you in the past. However, Ursula, you need to know that I will not be following that same pattern. If you intentionally destroy the things I get for you, then you will have to do without them. Furthermore, I will not tolerate your stomping through the house, nor you slamming doors around here, no matter how angry you get. If you become angry, Ursula, let's sit down and talk about what's wrong, and then come up with ways we can solve the issues. Ok?"

I was so shocked and mad at the same time that I couldn't even speak. I crossed my arms and sat back in the chair, turned my eyes from him and didn't bother to respond to that statement.

"May I go now?" I asked angrily.

"No you may not, Ursula; not yet." Dad stated.

"That birthday party you wanted to have, I don't think we will be doing that this year."

"What?!" I screamed. "No Party?! But it's my thirteenth birthday!"

"No, we won't be having a party this year," Dad insisted. "With how you treated your grandmother, and with your lack of appreciation for the things she bought you, do you actually think you deserve to celebrate your birthday with a party, Ursula?"

"Yes, I do!" I yelled back at him, so mad by now I could explode.

"I would like us to celebrate your birthday however; instead, I'd like us to do it with a private dinner. A celebration with just you and me would be very nice. You have my permission to invite one of your friends over as well. We will have cake, ice cream, your favorite foods, and we will go to your favorite arcade or a movie afterward -- your choice. I need to see improvement with your behavior, Ursula, before I can consider giving you a large birthday party celebration."

"You can keep your cake and ice cream! This isn't fair!" I yelled, now crying.

I got up, ran to my room, and got the bags of things he had just bought me. I stomped back to him and threw them on the floor in front of him. Now running back to my room, I couldn't believe this was happening. I had finally gotten one of my parents back and he's demanding this of me. It's his fault I behave the way I do in the first place. It's all his fault, and now he wants me to do all the changing!

"Well, I won't! I won't!" I said out loud. After slamming the door behind me again, I threw myself on the bed crying so hard I thought I would throw-up.

I knew what would make me feel better. I lifted my mattress and pulled out my pocket knife.

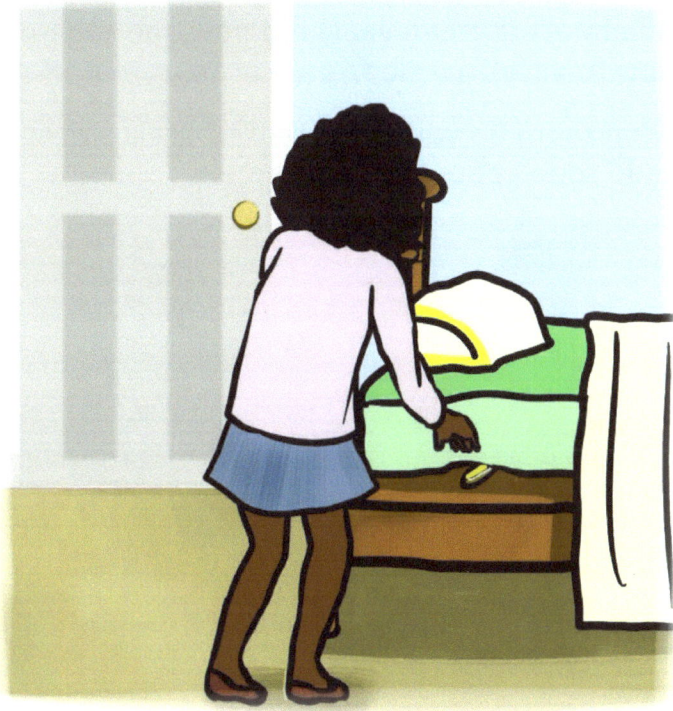

All of a sudden, there was a knock on my bedroom door.

Knock, knock, knock! I knew it was Dad. "Ursula, open this door, or I will use my key to come in," he said.

Oh, my goodness! I had to hide this knife. I stuck it under my mattress and got up to unlock the door. But I had to try to get rid of him first; at least long enough to do what I needed to do in order to make the pain inside my heart go away. At least long enough to use this knife.

"Dad, would you please leave me alone!" I screamed, hoping he would go away just long enough for me to do my Cutting.

"No ma'am, I will not. You have until I count to three to open this door, or I will do it myself!" and he began to count. "One -- two," I was unlocking the door by the time he said, "three."

"I'm almost thirteen years old now and can't even have any privacy!" I yelled.

"What more do you want, Dad?!" I said, wishing that he would soon get out of my room.

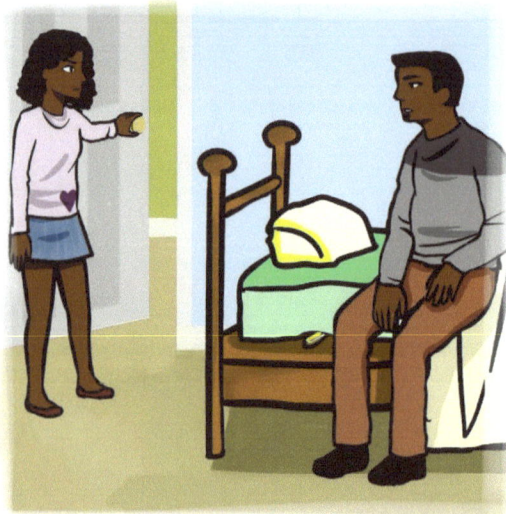

As Dad walked into the room I continued to stand at the door. He walked in and sat on my bed as he began to talk.

"Ok, Ursula. I understand you are not accustomed to anyone being this strict on you, but you have two minutes to go and pick up your packages you threw in that floor, or I'm taking your things back to the store. Your two minutes begin now."

Dad looked down at his watch, and I knew then that he was serious; but so was I. I didn't move. I guess we were both a lot alike. After what I knew had been two minutes, Dad walked out of my room. I could hear him picking up the mess I had made in the living room. I also heard the front door close and the car start.

Things were happening too fast. I couldn't think of the right scheme fast enough to outwit him. I just couldn't think. How could Dad possibly think that his little sob 'grown-up' story could make up for all the times I had spent hurting because neither my mom nor dad had really been in my life. All the times that they had *mother/daughter* dinners at school, and my mother was not there and grandma was too sick to attend with me. All the times when they had *daddy/daughter* dances at school, and my dad wasn't there. Daddy's little *speech* could never make up for the constant pain.

Oh, I'll figure this out later. Right now, I knew what I had to do. I needed to Cut. I needed to Cut, right now. I went to my mattress and pulled out my knife. I then traded one kind of pain for another kind of pain. Any new pain right now was better than having this piercing, stabbing, yet empty pain in my heart. As I watched the blood trickle down my arm, tears also saturated my face.

By the time Dad got back home, I had cleaned up myself, and even managed to calm down a little. However, I was still angry with Dad, and wasn't ready to face him again. He left me alone when he came in. I could hear him moving around in the kitchen, though. I guess he was preparing dinner. Several thoughts began to roll around in my mind. I had to figure out now if I was going to continue to be stubborn and refuse to eat dinner, or would I pretend nothing had happened, and come out of this room. I was very hungry by now, so the latter thought would have to take precedent.

Pretending nothing had happened was what I had decided to do; but it had happened. Now I had no new boots, and no new head set to show off at school. Absolutely nothing for my birthday, and now no birthday party either. When you get right down to it, I even think it was really all my fault. How stupid was that of me trying to outsmart my dad when I was the one losing out. We did seem to be two of a kind. I began to realize that life would start getting really rough if I didn't come up with a better strategy to out-smart Dad.

As I walked into the kitchen, I took a deep breath and said with not much enthusiasm, "Need some help with preparing dinner, Dad?"

He looked up from the sink where he was washing some fresh veggies and said with an actual smile on his face,

"Sure Ursula. Feeling better?"

Without him waiting for an answer, he handed me the veggies he had been washing and said,

"Put these in the boiling pot of water on the stove when you are finished, and be careful not to splash the hot water on yourself."

He then moved over to check on what was in the oven. We continued preparing dinner, set the table, and then we both sat down to eat. Needless to say, we ate in silence.

As we cleared the table together, Dad said,

"Oh yeah. Ursula, you will be going to school late tomorrow. I set a doctor's appointment for you to get a complete physical in the morning, and I will take you to school once you are finished."

"What?!" I shouted. "I don't need to see a doctor!"

I said, knowing very well that any physical examination would expose the cuts I had everywhere.

"Well, your grandmother said that you've been avoiding doctors for two years now. With you getting older, I'm sure there are some teenage girlie kinds of questions you must have by now," Dad said as though he was actually helping me out.

"If you feel comfortable enough, we can discuss anything you might have on your mind before we see the doctor tomorrow. Need to talk?" he asked very innocently.

Oh my goodness! I thought. What was I going to do?

"I have a very important test tomorrow at school I can't miss," I said quickly, knowing that I really didn't, but I had to come up with something!

"We are not rescheduling your physical exam, young lady. I'll call the school in the morning and ask them to reschedule your test." He said, not knowing that he would find out I didn't have a test at school tomorrow when he called.

Wow! What was I going to do? I felt as though my whole world was closing in on me and I had no way of escape. I started crying uncontrollably, and then I no longer felt my legs beneath me. Now, falling to the floor on my knees, I was completely out of answers. I didn't want to think about all of this anymore. All I could do was cry. My body started shaking and I couldn't control that either. It seemed that I wasn't even *me* anymore. A second later, I completely collapsed on the floor. My stomach was now in knots, and my head was pounding like a big brass band was marching between my ears. Dad was calling my name, I think. Now, nothing but blackness – quietness – no – more -- pain.

"Open your eyes, Ursula. Sweetie, come back to me. It's going to be alright. I'm here, Ursula. Open your eyes. Open your eyes."

I could hear my dad's voice, but it seemed far away. Now, it was getting louder. I opened my eyes and saw that he was leaning over me talking to me. I was in bed.

"Dad?" I asked, not sure of exactly what was going on.

"Welcome back, sweetie." He said, looking very concerned as he stared into my foggy eyes.

"We are at the hospital, sweetie. You passed out in the kitchen yesterday after dinner. This is Dr. McJenney. She will be helping us through some confusing issues," Dad told me, as I was still attempting to gain my mental and physical focus.

"Honey, we know about the cuts and the scars you have. I went home this morning after I knew you were stable, and searched your room. I found the pocket knife you had under your mattress. The police had to come with me because they weren't sure if I had been abusing you. Don't worry. You are not in trouble. We both just have some readjusting to do, but please know that you won't have to do this alone anymore. I will be here, healing right along with you, Ursula. I will never leave you alone again, Ok?"

All I could say was, "OK." I couldn't fight anymore. There was no more rebellion in me to continue that life I had made for myself -- to continue in that world of pain and loneliness. I was ready to discover the person I was meant to be. It couldn't have been the person I had become. I looked up at my dad and smiled a real smile that I don't think I'd ever experienced before. Now reaching for his hand, he grabbed mine, and leaned over my bed, giving me the most loving hug I think I have ever received. Dad kissed my forehead, and now we both were crying; but I was so happy. Me? Happy? I can't ever remember really being happy before. A feeling came over me that seemed just as foreign. I was in *no pain* -- absolutely, no pain. For the first time in my life that I could remember I felt no hurt and no pain anywhere -- not even in my heart!

I then looked up at Dr. McJenney and said, "I'm delighted to meet you, Dr. McJenney. When can we start?"

Through several sessions with Doctor McJenney, I was introduced to rubber bands. They are large colorful bands that you wear on your wrist. When you feel the urge to Cut, you simple snap the rubber band on your wrist instead. It creates a slight pain that doesn't leave a scar, but becomes a pretty good substitute for that distraction you are seeking when you Cut.

I have some now in multiple colors that match any outfit I'd be wearing. It's pretty cool actually.

Dad and I are learning new coping skills together now. I haven't cut in over six months. Even though I still have the evidence of destructive Cutting practices on my arms and upper legs, it's a reminder of a life that I don't intend to ever go back to. Dad has even agreed to allow me to start getting tattoos, as long as I stay clean of Cutting, and that I'm not getting it as a trade-off for some kind of stress resulting from anger. It's best to deal with that kind of stuff head on. We realize that I'm pretty young still; however, getting a tattoo every now and then is certainly a more positive alternative to what I used to do. My first one will be on the back side of my right shoulder. It's a picture of a butterfly to remind me of a totally new me -- a totally new life, and a totally new way of handling all kinds of challenging situations.

I'm going on sixteen years old now, and so far it's been a really cool adjustment that Dad and I can both agree upon. I've got a feeling that I'm going to be just fine.

Spirit of Truth Storybook
Activity Page

1. *After reading the story, ask yourself the following questions:*

   - What did you like about the story?

   - What would you change about the story?

   - What could you have done to make things turn out differently?

   - Can you think of a way to help others after reading this story?

2. *Go back through the story pages and **decode** your **secret message**.*

   - Write the message on the lines below.

   - Send it to me through my website at: www.BooksByLMason.com

I will send you back a personal comment. Be sure to include your gender and age.

S.O.T. Messages of Encouragement Worksheet

(Fill in the missing letters on a <u>separate sheet of paper</u> or here, if you own the storybook, to unlock your secret message)

Ungrateful Ursula

M _ _ _ _   _ h _ _   _ p p _ _ _ _   _ _

_ _   _ n g _ _ _ _ f _ _ _ e _ _   _ _ _ _ _

b _   _   s _ g _   _ _   _ i _ d _ _

_ n g _ _   _ _ _ _ l _   _ _ _ _   h _ _ _ _ _ .

_ _ _ _   o _ _   w _ _   _ _ u   _ _ _

_ _   a _ _ r _ ,   _ _ _ r _ _ s   _ _ ,

_ _ _   b _ _ _ _   t _   _ _ j _ _

_ _ _ _ _ _   a _ _   l _ _ _   _ g _ _ _ .

3. If there are puppets in your book, cut out the
   finger puppets and assemble as instructed. Be
   careful with your scissors.

- Use your finger to help the
  character walk out a happy scene
  that you create

- When finished playing, place
  your puppet characters in a zip lock bag
  or an envelope, and store it between your
  favorite pages of the book, for safe keeping.

- Ask your parent or guardian if you can
  collect all 26 "Spirit of Truth Storybook
  Series" and remember to save the *Dove
  Cutouts* and glue them into the proper
  places on the chart.

Dove Cut Out Letter

Receive *15% discount coupon* off of the purchase of my Editor's Edition of "**The Spirit of Truth**" Storybook Series, with proof of purchase from A - Z. This special edition will contain all 26 stories within one volume along with some added goodies. Fill out the chart below and **please print** all information clearly.

A	B	C	D	E	F
G	H	I	J	K	L
M	N	O	P	Q	R
S	T	U	V	W	X
Y	Z				

Glue your "*Dove Letter*" cutouts in the corresponding boxes, on top of the proper letter. Fill 26 spaces from A- Z. Then cut this page out and mail it to:

Linda Mason
P. O box 1162
Powhatan, VA 23139

Name _____

Address _____

State _____ **Zip** _____ **Email** _____

Ungrateful Ursula's Brain Game #1
Visual Activity

Can you find the 9 items out of place on this picture? List them on the lines on the next page under Brain Game # 1.

Brain Game's Activity Worksheet

Brain Game #1

1._____

2._____

3._____

4._____

5._____

6._____

7._____

8._____

9._____

Ungrateful Ursula's Brain Game #2
Visual Activity

Ursula is really mad now as she leaves her dad's car. I think she's dreaming. Can you find the 8 things out of place in this dream? Place your answers on the worksheet that follows.

Brain Game's Activity Worksheet

Brain Game #2

1._____

2._____

3._____

4._____

5._____

6._____

7._____

8._____

Master Brain Game Answer Keys

Ungrateful Ursula #1	Ungrateful Ursula #2
Tiger tail	Rainbow
Bee	Fish
Ketchup	Large paperclip
Pie	Bird
Flying pig	Spider
Ghost	Snorkel
Flower	Grass Skirt
Cat	Pencil in hair
Cheese slice	

**APPROPRIATE AGE LEVEL
COLOR CODING KEY**

The reading level for these stories is grade 5, but they can be understood and enjoyed by younger children, when read to them by older children or adults. The storybook covers have been colored to reflect the average comprehension levels for the following age groups.

**Ages 4 and 5 = GREEN COVERS
Ages 6 and 7 = BLUE COVERS
Ages 8 and 9 = ORANGE COVERS
Ages 10 and above = RED COVERS**

*A special inspirational message has been coded throughout each story to help create 'added focus,' as well as, a visual tool for interactive concentration. **Decode your secret message (written in red lettering throughout the story)** and send it to me, along with your name and age, through my personal email address on my website at www.BooksByLMason.com and you will receive a personal email response from me. Some of the letters of the secret message have already been provided to assist you in your decoding. Additionally, <u>an added bonus</u> finger puppet activity, brain games, puzzles or other goodies, awaits each reader in the back of every storybook. An added "Treasure Hunt" can be found throughout the illustrations from my collection of storybooks, **<u>which details of this treasure hunt can only be found on my website.</u>***

Also, E-Book Editions of this collection of storybooks, having no activities in the back of the books, as well as A Collector's Edition of this 26 Storybook Series is forthcoming. The collector's edition will include all 26 stories in the same book or 2 Volumes; at which time, the Master's List of every inspirational message will be revealed.

1. *Anxious Arlene:* This story is about an *anxious* family consisting of a young brother and sister who lives with their grandpa and grandma. They have a little adopted dog that was never claimed or found by the original owner, and they all live together (with a few mishaps), in a loving, exciting home. This story can be enjoyed by children ages five and up.

2. *Busy Benny:* This story is about a busy little boy who loves to tinker with Wacky car models. He gets the opportunity to create a child sized Wacky car, with the help of his mom and dad, and finally enters it into a race with him doing the driving. He runs into a little surprise during his test run. This story can be enjoyed by children ages seven and up.

3. *Catty Carla:* This story is about a group of neighborhood house cats who carry on 'catty' conversations behind their friend's back at times. One particular Burmese cat soon realizes that her behavior was not appropriate, and it could be a little late for apologies. This story deals with death portrayed through animal characters. This book is dedicated to my daughter, Tamara, who as an adult, loss a cat she adored, Dr. Jeckyl, to an illness. The story line is very light; however, use parental wisdom. This story can be enjoyed by children ages five and up.

4. *Doubtful Denise:* This story is about a single father raising a young teenaged daughter who is full of doubt about herself, her abilities, and her future. Through a father's persistent encouragement and unyielding love for her, she eventually gains trust in herself and finds hope for a brighter future. This story can be enjoyed by children ages seven and up.

5. *Excited Ernesto:* This story is about a teenaged boy overcoming a fear of riding roller coasters. He experiences some exciting events at the county fair with a buddy friend of his and his buddy's sister, Maria. She adds extra excitement for Ernesto because no one knew she would be there, and he has a secret crush on her. Join this exciting group of youth as they sample the tasty treats found at all State Fairs, and as they experience some of the thrills of riding a roller coaster for the first time. Ride along with Ernesto, as your heart races to the beat of his own. This story can be enjoyed by children ages seven and up.

6. *Fearless Freddie:* Freddie is a little boy who is very creative and willing to test out any new adventure, regardless of risk. He is always ready and willing to try dangerous stunts until one day it gets him into big trouble. Does he learn from making dangerous choices, or does he continue to believe he is *invincible?* This story can be enjoyed by children ages five and up.

7. *Graceful Gregory:* Gregory loves to dance. He encounters teasing by his peers, but continues to do what he loves. He eventually meets another little boy who is not so interested in dancing, but his family is insisting that he gives it a try. The two boys meet and things begin to change for both of them. This story can be enjoyed by children ages seven and up, but younger if the reader is already dancing.

8. *Hopeful Henry:* Henry is full of anticipation for the new school year and is hopeful he will not experience the disappointments he has had in the past. He apparently gets disappointed over, and over again until a tragedy occurs in his life and he ends up being supported by the very people he thought were insignificant. He learns also, not only to see things differently, but to always be grateful and remain hopeful. This story can be enjoyed by children ages seven and up.

9. *Itchy Irvin:* This story is played out using a pack of dogs as characters. One of them misjudges some physical symptoms of another dog, and begins teasing him. That dog gets picked on constantly because of a skin condition. This particular *pack of dogs* meets a little boy who is going through a similar situation with his classmates at school. Let's see how this doggy story barks out. This story can be enjoyed by children ages seven and up.

10. *Jumping Josey:* This story is about a teenager who lives a life of thrills, while flipping and jumping, every chance she gets. She ultimately gets to experience one of her life's dreams -- sky diving. Travel with Josey as she goes on the most exhilarating jump of her life. This story can be enjoyed by children ages seven and up.

11. *Kissing Kirkland:* This story is about a very affectionate little boy who spends his days and nights kissing all kinds of creatures. Eventually, his normal kissing routine lands him into big trouble when he gets attacked by a momma duck. Let's follow our adorable *Kissing Kirkland* through an average day at home and see how he survives some of the repercussions having a personality like this, may present. This story can be enjoyed by children ages five and up.

12. *Lonely Lucilia:* This story is about two teenagers that are best friends. They are forced to separate, due to a family relocation, to a different country. The storyline starts out in a coastal town in Fife, Scotland, where Lucilia and Dillard have lived all of their lives. Take this lonesome journey with Lucilia, as she is forced to move from the only place she's ever known, and from her very best friend in the world, to a strange country she knows nothing about -- the United States of America. This story can be enjoyed by children ages eight and up.

13. *Muddy Maria:* This story explores the life of a little girl who loves to get dirty. With the help of her creative mother, her *dirty,* playful habit is channeled into a very productive fun activity. Dive in to this interesting twist of events and discover how playing in a lot of dirt, in some situations, can possibly turn out to be good for you. This story can be enjoyed by children ages five and up.

14. *Noisy Nelly:* This story explores the hatching of a bird from a bird's perspective. As this special bird explores her new world, words of wisdom flow from its mother. These words eventually take root in Nelly's heart in a very unique way. Soar with Nelly as she learns a very important lesson by refocusing her perspective on a part of her life she once perceived as gloomy. This story is dedicated to my first grandchild, Niyah Nylliana Mason, whom I believe one day will also soar as high as an eagle. This story can be enjoyed by children ages seven and up.

15. *Orphaned Ophelia:* Most of this story takes place in a very unique orphanage. Ophelia lives with the discomforts of not having a traditional family, but through it all she finds the compassion to help others. One day that compassion is returned, and she receives the most rewarding surprise of her life. This story can be enjoyed by children ages five and up.

16. *Pudgy Pete:* This story is about a little boy who obviously, because of his nickname, carries a little more weight than the average child. Journey with Pete as his self-pity and low self-esteem evolves into self-worth. After befriending a new *physically challenged* neighbor who moves in next door, she teaches him how to appreciate the special person he is, and not to focus on what size pants he wears. This story can be enjoyed by children ages seven and up.

17. *Quarrelsome Quaniqua:* This story contains **sensitive** material. It is not intended to be read as a *bedtime* story. Our story deals with a serious issue that some children must live with every day: ***an abusive living environment*** (non-sexual)***.*** The main character is a Latino teen (Quaniqua) who lives in poor, none-nurturing conditions. She becomes bitter and her behavior follows suit, until she meets someone outside of the home, and of a different culture, who finally treats her with respect. This causes Quaniqua to pull herself up and out of the pit she seemed to be falling into. Hang in there with her through the hard times, and see this young lady become a more productive, happier citizen. This story can be enjoyed by children eight and up; however, use parental wisdom as to if this story is suited for your particular younger child.

18. *Reckless Ricardo:* This story is about a young boy who starts out with some very reckless and disrespectful behaviors, but ends up with a very unusual science project that helps him start behaving in new, more respectful ways. You might be surprised at the results of this nontraditional outcome to a very common allergy. This story can be enjoyed by children ages seven and up.

19. Shy Stanley: This story is about a very quiet little boy who has some very interesting talents. He spends a lot of his time alone; however, he is extremely observant. Stanley meets a little girl with similar gifts and interests, which creates a bond that opens them both up to view their world differently. Let's visit these interesting young people and discover what their talents are. Maybe you have similar talents as well, and might have some interesting ideas of your own as to how to present those talents to the world. This story can be enjoyed by children ages seven and up.

20. *Tearful Tanya*: This story deals with a little girl who is full of grief over the passing of her grandmother. The family has a spiritual upbringing, and the little girl's mom guides her through the grieving process as she draws strength from above, where she's convinced her grandmother now resides. This story may be a little sensitive if you are a child in a similar situation, yet it can be enjoyed by children ages five and above.

21. *Ungrateful Ursula*: This story contains '**sensitive**' material. It is recommended for children ages ten and above. The story deals with a teenaged girl who grew up without her mother, and who very rarely saw her father. She lives temporarily with her aging grandmother. However, because of her grandmother's illness, Ursula must now live with her father, and she begins to use '*cutting*' as her method of coping. Things smooth out, but it's a very bumpy, painful ride. Walk with Ursula as she moves from '*much pain*' to '*much gain.*' This story can be enjoyed and read by children ages ten and above.

22. *Valiant Vivica*: This story is about a very gifted little girl who loves contact sports. Boys her same age seem to both admire her, and can be intimidated by her unprecedented strength at the same time. A natural disaster occurs on the day of Vivica's first wrestling tournament, and her valiant personality takes over. Follow along as she demonstrates extraordinary acts of bravery, and through it all, this experience will change her forever. This story can be enjoyed by children ages eight and above.

23. *Worrying Winston*: This story is about a little boy whose mother is an active Marine in the United States' Armed Forces. Winston is a very responsible little boy; however, he does worry a great deal about his mother's well-being. While on a *Treasure Hunt*, a game designed by his mother using riddles written in a letter Winston received, an unfortunate accident occurs and his mother ends up with a serious injury. Will they complete the Treasure Hunt? Stand with Winston and his father as they draw strength from each other to deal with a life's situation that changes their entire world. This story can be enjoyed by children ages eight and above.

24. *X-Con Xavier*: This story has been presented in '***limerick style poetry***' to lighten the seriousness of the topic for a child. Because of Xavier's destructive behavior, he is placed in various state institutions. Xavier meets a person while incarcerated that offers him hope and a different way of thinking. His inner spiritual change eventually points him in a new direction. Now with new hope, he has a chance to begin a new, more productive lifestyle outside of lock-up. This story can be enjoyed and read by children ages ten and above.

25. *Yearning Yolanda*: This story takes you on a short journey with a twelve year old young girl who lost her eyesight in a car accident a year ago. She yearns for life to be as it was before the accident; however, life has a way of throwing you constant challenges that could cause you to either withdraw further into bitterness, or to emerge with a heart of gratefulness. Which one will Yolanda choose? Walk with Yolanda through an even harder challenge that, if handled with fear and bitterness, could not only take her life, but the lives of her mother and her best friend, Toby (her dog). This story can be enjoyed by children ages eight and above.

26. *Zealous Zeporah*: Zeporah is a very passionate young lady full of enthusiasm for life. She jogged regularly, but one day she slipped and fell injuring her ankle. A situation such as this would have brought most people to a halt, or perhaps could cause others to go into a state of temporary depression. How will Zeporah handle a situation like this, when so many people are depending on her enthusiasm to help motivate them? This story can be enjoyed by children ages seven and above.

41

About The Author

Minister Linda Mason is a unique ministry gift to the Body of Christ. Her experiences include the establishment of *Spirit of Praise Liturgical Outreach, Inc.*, a non-profit 501 © 3 organization, which not only helped to establish and oversee new dance ministries, but also extended into the communities.

In addition to the *Spirit of Truth Storybook Series*, Minister Linda has published *Appetizers from the Word of God... Are You Hungry?* Volumes 1, 2, & 3; which is an awesome tool for teaching foundational truths, in a simplistic manner, from God's Word.

Linda is a native of Suffolk, Virginia, the wife of George B. Mason, Jr., the mother of three; Tamara, Tiena, and George III. She has two adorable grandchildren, Niyah and Laana. Linda holds an Associate Degree in Early Childhood Education and has a passion for writing. She has written and is in the process of publishing these 26 children's stories from A to Z. Her plan is to have these unique stories available in both English and Spanish in the near future.

What others have stated about this Series

- *Author Linda Mason's book, "Kissing Kirkland", is one of a series of books that tells a delightful story with a secret hidden valuable message for children. Her stories will captivate her audience with a variety of age appropriate activities to enhance each child's learning. As an educator for many years, I highly recommend her books!* **By Amelia Hopkins, a high school counselor.**

- *Linda Mason has done an excellent job using her creativity and insight in writing this series of books, the* ***Spirit of Truth Storybook Series from A-Z****. Each book deals with a subject or situation, such as a particular disability, or set-back that a child might encounter and have difficulty dealing with. The books offer resolutions that are positive and encouraging, helping a child build strength, confidence and maturity. The activities in the back of each book reinforce the lesson learned. The graphics are colorful and eye-catching, and each book's vocabulary is age appropriate. Each book is color coded to fit each age group, so there are appropriate books for every child's age. These are books your children will want to read or hear over and over; read by a big sister or brother. And they also have the opportunity to communicate with the author directly! I highly recommend these books for your children and grandchildren!* **By Nona J. Mason, a retired teacher, mother and grandmother.**

www.ingramcontent.com/pod-product-compliance
Lightning Source LLC
Chambersburg PA
CBHW042125080426
42733CB00002B/13